LOVE TALK

WORKBOOK FOR MEN

D0449970

Speak Each Other's
Language Like You
Never Have Before

DRS. LES & LESLIE PARROTT

ZONDERVAN®

ZONDERVAN.com/
AUTHORTRACKER
follow your favorite authors

Love Talk Workbook for Men
Copyright © 2004 by Les and Leslie Parrott

Requests for information should be addressed to:

Zondervan, *Grand Rapids, Michigan 49530*

ISBN-10: 0-310-26212-7
ISBN-13: 978-0-310-26212-1

Published in association with INJOY, Inc., Duluth, Georgia.

Interior design by Michelle Espinoza

Printed in the United States of America

Contents

A LETTER TO OUR READERS

We've always enjoyed this quote from comedian Woody Allen: "I took a speed reading course and read *War and Peace* in twenty minutes. It involves Russia."

Ever felt like that after reading a book? We have. Sometimes it becomes so easy to focus on finishing a book that we miss its main message. What you hold in your hand is a kind of insurance policy against that happening while you are reading *Love Talk*. But it's more than that.

Books let us shake hands with new ideas. But these ideas remain as flat as the printed page if we do not apply them to our lives. For this reason, we have designed workbooks—one for men and one for women—that will help you incorporate into your relationship the new lessons you learn while reading. And we've designed them to be used either individually or in a small group setting.

For Individual and Couple Study

As you read through the main book, you will discover places where it points you to do an exercise in these workbooks. Most of them are designed for you to take about five or ten minutes on your own to complete a few questions or to take a brief self-test and then compare your results with your partner (which is why it's important to each have your own workbook). Or it may give you an exercise to do together so you can put a new principle into practice. This is where real learning occurs. This is where new ideas become more than acquaintances; they begin to make a positive difference in your marriage.

We have used these exercises with countless couples, both in our counseling practice as well as in our seminar settings. They are proven. They work. And that's why we are passionate about you doing them as you read through our book.

While there is no one right way to use these workbooks, we suggest you complete the exercises as you encounter them in the book, or soon after you have finished reading the chapter that covers the exercise. In other words, try to complete the exercises for that chapter before moving on to the next one. The point is to integrate the exercises into the process of reading the book.

For Small Group Couple's Study

In the appendix of this workbook you'll find a small group study guide designed specifically for you to use with other couples. Research shows that one of the most effective ways to internalize new content and gain new insight is by discussing the material with others. And when it comes to learning more about communication in marriage, this is especially true. That's why we've designed a small group DVD for just such a purpose. It includes six sessions with conversational jump starts and lots of practical application to help your group get the most from *Love Talk*.

As you go through this workbook, you will see that a few of the exercises are designated to work well in small group sessions. In other words, while you will want to do them on your own, they will serve as a great jumping off place for small group discussion and interaction. The DVD will direct you on how to use these specific exercises in your sessions.

In addition to using some of the workbook exercises in your small group session, you will also want to use the associated discussion questions found in the appendix for each of your six sessions together.

Whether you are using these workbooks individually or in a small group setting, we hope that as you proceed through these pages you'll make it your own. Don't get too hung up on following the rules. If a particular exercise leads you down a more intriguing path, take it. Some of these exercises may simply serve as springboards to discussions that fit your style more appropriately. However, if an exercise seems a bit challenging, don't give up on it. As the saying goes, anything worth having is worth working for—especially when it comes to our relationships.

So whether you are a speed learner or not, we hope you don't approach *Love Talk* just to check it off your to-do list. We pray that you will, instead, use these exercises, self-tests, and discussion questions to internalize the message of *Love Talk* and fortify your relationship by speaking each other's language like you never have before.

GETTING WHERE
YOU WANT TO GO

Someone once said that the achievement of your goal is assured the moment you commit yourself to it. We certainly agree with that. But long before a commitment to a goal is made, one must thoroughly understand his goal. So in this first exercise we challenge you to drill down deep on this thought. We want you to give serious consideration to where you would like to be as a result of completing *Love Talk*. We have a few ways, right off the top, to help you do just that.

Begin by perusing the following list of potential goals as they relate to communication. Circle any and all that pertain to you. Of course, jot down the goal you may have that is not in this list.

- Be a better listener.
- Stay on point.
- Don't finish my partner's sentences.
- Curb my emotions when talking.
- Be more sensitive to my partner's feelings.
- Think clearly before speaking.
- Avoid jumping to conclusions.
- Tune in to and discern my partner's emotions.
- Maintain eye contact while talking.
- Be more vulnerable.
- Be more comfortable with conflict.
- Speak with more clarity.

- Invite and receive feedback.
- Use more humor.
- Come across personally warmer.
- Express more genuine interest.
- Be more assertive with my needs.
- Better assess when to talk.
- Don't jump to conclusions.

Once you have circled the ones that pertain to you, note a specific time and place where you'd like to see that improvement. For example, if you circled "Be a better listener," you may write next to it that you'd like to do that when your partner is talking about her day at work or maybe when she is talking about her mother. The point is to be specific so you can actually recognize and measure your improvement on this goal. So go back to this list now and write something beside the items you circled to make them more specific.

Next, consider the following five realms of communication and indicate on each of the scales where you see yourself on it. Be thoughtful and honest as you answer.

Information Sharing: Stating your thoughts and feelings with accuracy and clarity without getting sidetracked or embroiled in emotion.

Weak   Strong

1   2   3   4   5   6   7   8   9   10

Listening: Paying respectful attention to the content and feelings of another in a way that they know they have been accurately understood.

Weak   Strong

1   2   3   4   5   6   7   8   9   10

Conflict management: Being aware of conflict and employing methods to diffuse it and move beyond it.

Weak   Strong

1   2   3   4   5   6   7   8   9   10

Problem solving: Working out effective steps with one another to effectively and efficiently reach a desired state.

Weak   Strong

1   2   3   4   5   6   7   8   9   10

Skill selection: Determining which communication skills are most useful at specific times.

Weak   Strong

1   2   3   4   5   6   7   8   9   10

Once you have rated yourself on each of these five scales, you may want to have your partner rate you on these same items. This can heighten your self-awareness as you begin to articulate your communication goals.

Finally, in this exercise, write down two or three specific goals. Consider what you have done in the above exercise. Be specific. The more specific the better.

Goal 1: _____

_____

_____

Goal 2: _____

_____

_____

Goal 3: _____

_____

_____

Now that you have put your specific goals in writing, be aware of the huge step you have just taken. Only a very small percentage of people put their goals in writing—but those who do are more than twice as likely to reach them as those who just talk about them. And what's more, those who review their goals from time to time are ten times more likely to achieve them. So throughout *Love Talk,* we recommend that you revisit the goals to see how what you have just learned is bringing you closer to them.

Congratulations! You are off to a great start.

ASSESSING YOUR COMMUNICATION IQ

This assessment will give you a general idea of how you are doing when it comes to the basics of communication. Answer these simple questions as honestly as you can.

1. T F What I say is more important than how I say it.
2. T F When we are in sync, my partner should be able to almost read my mind.
3. T F The basic goal of good communication in a loving relationship is to convey information accurately.
4. T F The children's rhyme is right: "Words can never hurt you."
5. T F If you're not talking, you're not communicating.
6. T F The best communicators accurately get their point across first, then they try to understand their partner.
7. T F Using "I" statements (rather than "you" statements) is self-centered.
8. T F Good relational communication between partners always involves logical thinking.
9. T F Physical touch is a low-level priority in effective communication between partners.
10. T F Communication differences between men and women are relatively minor.

_____ Total true answers

_____ Total false answers

If you have eight or more false answers, you are well on your way to having the basics of good talk under your belt, and you are primed to benefit significantly from Love Talk. If your score isn't that high, don't feel bad. You're not alone and will probably benefit from a quick brushup on the fundamentals outlined in the next chapter of the book. There you will find an easy-to-read overview of the most important skills required for good communication.

But even if you scored a perfect 10 out of 10 on this assessment, you probably still encounter conversations between you and your partner that fall flat. So the quick review of a few fundamentals in the next chapter will likely benefit you as well.

A note of caution: The point of this exercise is to get a quick idea of where you are on the fundamentals. It's not about scoring better than your partner. It's not a competition. So if you scored higher than she did, take the higher ground and don't make an issue out of it.

YOUR CURRENT COUPLE-COMMUNICATION STRENGTHS

The rare couple periodically articulates what they do well as a team. Think about it: most couples are more prone to complain about their pitfalls than they are to praise themselves for their successes. If we aren't careful, we're likely to exchange pep rallies for gripe sessions. Don't fall into this temptation—especially as it relates to your ability to communicate.

In this exercise we want you to take stock of what's working and what's not in the area of your communication. Be sure to do this separately, each of you in your own workbook, before you compare notes.

Begin by reviewing the list below and checking which things you do well and which things your partner does well. Once you have done this, review your column of check marks and note which items you both do well and which items neither of you does particularly well. Feel free to add to this list any communication abilities you think are missing for you. And, as always, the more honest you are, the more helpful this exercise will be to you.

Who does this well ...	You	Her	Both	Neither
Listening without interruption	❑	❑	❑	❑
Staying on topic	❑	❑	❑	❑
Ready to apologize	❑	❑	❑	❑

	You	Her	Both	Neither
Controlling emotions appropriately	❏	❏	❏	❏
Giving full attention	❏	❏	❏	❏
Identifying and expressing feelings	❏	❏	❏	❏
Thinking clearly before speaking	❏	❏	❏	❏
Reserving opinion until the right time	❏	❏	❏	❏
Maintaining eye contact while talking	❏	❏	❏	❏
Being appropriately vulnerable	❏	❏	❏	❏
Permitting productive conflict	❏	❏	❏	❏
Speaking with clarity	❏	❏	❏	❏
Inviting and receiving feedback	❏	❏	❏	❏
Using humor appropriately	❏	❏	❏	❏
Coming accross as personally warm	❏	❏	❏	❏
Expressing more genuine interest	❏	❏	❏	❏
Being assertive with needs	❏	❏	❏	❏
Knowing when to talk and when not to	❏	❏	❏	❏
_____	❏	❏	❏	❏
_____	❏	❏	❏	❏

The above items you checked for both you and your partner are your "current couple-communication strengths." The items that neither of you does particularly well are your "current couple-communication deficits." You will undoubtedly compare numbers, and that's okay. But don't get hung up on which list is longer or shorter. That's not the point of this exercise. Here we simply want you to become aware of what you are doing well.

So compare notes in each other's workbooks and see which items you both agree are your current communication strengths. In other words, review the checklists you have done separately to see which items both of you said were things you both do well. If you don't have any at this point, relax. That's okay too. And if you have several, good for you! All we are concerned about at this point is taking inventory.

One more thing. Notice that these are "current" strengths. In other words, this is not how it will always be. We plan on adding many more strengths to your list by the time you have completed *Love Talk*.

LET'S GET REAL

Attending skills. That's what experts call the ability to be genuine in conversation. It's living in the moment. Being fully present. It's the ability to give your physical and psychological attention to your partner. Effective attending skills are the nonverbal expressions of profound interest and attention toward your partner. We all like to be on the receiving end of good attending skills.

In this exercise we want you to explore your own attending skills and see how effective you are with each of these skills. Below are the ingredients that make up the expression of genuineness in conversation. Rate your ability on each of the continuums.

Positive Eye Contact

This is not a fixed stare, but an easy, natural gaze that provides comfort and understanding. If you are particularly proficient in this, you do not become distracted and divert your gaze to gather surrounding information; instead, you focus in on your partner with a genuine interest. In your conversations, how often do you exhibit good eye contact? What percentage of the time do you do this?

| 0 | 10 | 20 | 30 | 40 | 50 | 60 | 70 | 80 | 90 | 100 |

Open and Inviting Posture

This is more than facing your partner while conversing. Usually when you are listening with a genuine heart, you lean slightly toward the person speaking to you. You remain relaxed but your posture is open, indicating that you are mentally receptive to what is being said. What percentage of the time do you do this?

0   10   20   30   40   50   60   70   80   90   100

Tuned-In Gestures

One of the ways we know that another person is genuinely interested in us is by the absence of distracting and fidgety gestures. Body movements convey volumes about how much a person really wants to talk to us. If you drum your fingers on the chair, crack your knuckles, clean your glasses, stretch your neck, sneak a look at your watch, or anything along these lines, you are not conveying genuine interest (even thought you may feel genuinely interested). How much of the time in conversation with your partner do you avoid making distracting gestures?

0   10   20   30   40   50   60   70   80   90   100

Interested Silence

A period of active, attentive silence serves as a gentle nudge to your partner to move deeper into the conversation. It allows her time to think and reflect and then comfortably proceed. In other words, when you practice interested silence, you allow your partner to proceed at her own pace. How often do you practice this ability in conversation with your partner?

0   10   20   30   40   50   60   70   80   90   100

Simply rating yourself on this skill set gives you a good idea of your ability to be genuine with your partner. We must tell you, however, that most people will rate themselves higher on each of these than their spouses would rate them. So you can expand this exercise by having your partner rate where she thinks you are on each of these qualities. If you elect to do this, we urge you to do so in a spirit of accurate understanding—not accusation. The goal is to improve by becoming more self-aware, not to feel bad about yourself or to jab your partner. We'll leave this portion of the exercise up to you. If you both agree, go for it. But if one of you would rather pass, we suggest you leave it alone.

FINDING THE TIME TO TALK

Someone once said that the one thing you can't recycle is wasted time. How true. But you can often find more time for what matters most—if you are willing to look for it. Accurately assessing how you spend your time in an average week is the key to finding more time. Each week is made up of 168 hours. How does it divvy up for you? Completing the following items will show you.

Number of hours you sleep each night _____ x 7 = _____

Number of hours you work (or attend school) each week _____

Number of hours per day spent on food preparation and eating _____ x 7 = _____

Number of hours per day spent on grooming _____ x 7 = _____

Number of hours per day spent on exercise _____ x 7 = _____

Number of hours per day spent on commuting _____ x 7 = _____

Number of hours per day spent on entertainment (watching TV, playing video games, surfing the Web, reading, etc.) _____ x 7 = _____

Number of hours per day spent on socializing with friends (and caring for children if you are a parent) _____ x 7 = _____

Number of hours per day spent on email and phone outside of work _____ x 7 = _____

Number of hours per day spent cleaning or doing chores _____ x 7 = _____

Now add up the totals: _____

Subtract the above number from 168–_____ = _____

These are the remaining hours you have for one-on-one time with your partner.

Now that you've identified how you spend most of your time, consider these questions as a starter for creating more time together:

- Does the amount of time you have for talking with your partner surprise you? Why?

- If you want to find more time together, what can you do? What can you realistically change in your schedule to permit this?

- Even if you have time together, it may not be "quality" time. Why? If it's not, what can you do to increase the level of quality time you have together?

- The 80–20 Rule was originally stated by the Italian economist Vilfredo Pareto: "80 percent of the reward comes from 20 percent of the effort." How would you identify the valuable 20 percent that brings you and your partner closer together?

- Have you talked about your biological prime time? That's the time of day when you are at your best. Knowing when your best time is can help you optimize your one-on-one time together. Are you a "morning person," a "night owl," or a late afternoon "whiz"? If you are out of sync with each other's biological prime time, what can you do to compensate for that?

YOUR THREE LEVELS
OF COMMUNICATION

Aren't you just a little curious about the amount of time you spend at each of the three levels of communication? Well, let's quit wondering and do our best to identify just how much of our conversation with our partner is spent at each. Take a moment to review the three levels and then draw a pie chart in the circle on page 24—a pie chart that represents your best guess at how much of your conversation with your partner in a given week is at the grunt level, the journalist level, or the feelings level.

The Grunt Level

Involves little more than obligatory comments. The requisite "How ya doing?" is met with the predictable "Fine." That's it.

The Journalist Level

Involves facts and opinions about such topics as politics, people, the church, movies, or sports. "Isn't it time the Smiths take down their Christmas lights?" Just reporting and discussing, but that's where it stops. This level lacks intimacy.

The Feelings Level

Involves a deep sense of safety in which one can share insecurities. "I really felt inadequate at work today." One's guard is let down and heart is revealed—all in a context of understanding and acceptance.

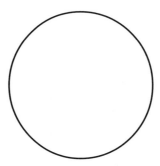

Once you have done your best to divvy up your circle into these three levels, compare notes with your partner. Discuss your inevitable discrepancies—remembering to do so with calm compassion. This is an exercise in understanding, not judging. Explore questions of when and where each of you is most likely to cultivate the feelings level of conversation. When you both agree on a time and place when this kind of conversation is most likely to occur between the two of you, you will have identified your sweet spot for good conversation. That's important! Write down the times and places you are most likely to have a feelings-level talk:

_____

_____

_____

_____

The sweet spots of conversation you have just identified can serve as a kind of safe house in your relationship. You can't expect all of your conversations to be deep and safe, but you can know of occasions just around the next bend when they will be—as long as you are looking for them.

AVOIDING UNWANTED ADVICE

Advice is so deadly to most conversations that it should really be treated like a telegram—something that you get or give on rare occasions. This exercise will help you curb your compulsive advice-giving, if that's a problem for you, and make this fundamental skill much more intentional.

Identify three areas where you are least likely to want advice. These may include doing something you do routinely (sweep the porch), something you do for enjoyment (crossword puzzle), something you do in your own style (parallel park), and so forth. You get the idea. Note two or three of these for you.

1. _____
2. _____
3. _____

When are you most likely to want advice? What are the areas where you welcome your partner's input and suggestions? Maybe it's on the things she does better than you. Note those here.

1. _____
2. _____
3. _____

Once you have completed these two lists, share them with your partner and compare notes. Talk about any that surprised you on each other's lists. Reveal to each other what you learned as a result—what's new to you.

Next, we want to challenge you to do something a bit tougher. Focus on your own advice-giving. When are you most likely to give advice to your partner? Maybe you give advice on something predictable (how to grill a hamburger), something she does that frustrates you (how not to lose car keys), or something that you do without thinking (how to drive). Identify two or three of these specific situations when you tend to be most prone to giving your partner advice.

1. _____

2. _____

3. _____

Now, in a single sentence, write out why you think you give your partner advice. In other words, what motivates you to do so?

_____

_____

The point of this exercise is to help each of you empathize with your advice-giving. The more you understand where each of you is coming from on giving advice, the more grace you will have to receive it when it comes your way and to curb it when you are likely to dole it out.

IDENTIFYING YOUR
PERSONAL FEAR FACTOR

This exercise will help you zero in on what is most likely to be your single greatest stumbling block you will ever encounter to speaking each other's language. It is what holds you and your partner back from consistently enjoying the kind of conversations you both long for. It's your fear factor.

As you learned in *Love Talk*, research has revealed four primary fears we encounter in the daily exchange of our relationship. They have to do with what you fear losing: time, approval, loyalty, or quality. Rank them in order (1 being your greatest fear):

I fear losing . . .

_____ time (I don't want to waste it).

_____ approval (I don't want to put people off).

_____ loyalty (I don't want to jeopardize continuity).

_____ quality (I don't want to tarnish my good reputation).

Now that you have ranked this list of potential fear factors, consider how you think your partner might do this same thing and indicate that here:

My partner most fears losing . . .

_____ time (she doesn't want to waste it).

_____ approval (she doesn't want to put people off).

_____ loyalty (she doesn't want to jeopardize continuity).

_____ quality (she doesn't want to tarnish her good reputation).

Okay, you've guessed it: now it's time for the two of you to compare lists. Find out how accurately each of you identified what you see as your biggest fear factor. Here are some questions that may guide your discussion:

- What do you see as my biggest fear factor and why?
- What real-life examples or experiences did you base your answer on?
- What have we learned about each other's top emotional security needs that we didn't know before this exercise?
- If we know each other's perceived fear factors, how might we approach our conversations differently? How might we use this information to improve them?

IDENTIFYING YOUR TALK STYLE

If you have access to the Internet, we strongly recommend that you take advantage of the Love Talk Indicator (available at www.RealRelation ships.com). This online assessment is sure to be an eye-opener that will reveal far more than a workbook exercise. Of course, you can still use this exercise to generate positive discussion regarding the results. And if you do not have access to the online Love Talk Indicator, you can still make significant progress through this exercise.

You've learned about the four essential questions required for speaking Love Talk. And chances are you've already given each one some serious consideration. Here, we want you to take a moment to place an *M* (for "me") along each of the following continuums to indicate where you see yourself.

How You Tackle Problems

Aggressively   Passively

How You Influence Your Partner

Feelings   Facts

How You React to Change

Aggressively   Passively

How You Make Decisions

Feelings   Facts

Now revisit each of these four continuums and place a *P* (for "partner") on each one where you think your partner is most likely to land. It may be quite close to your *M* in some cases and far away in others.

Once you have plotted where you believe both you and your partner are individually on these continuums, compare notes. Explore why each of you answered as you did. Talk about what surprised you and why.

This brief exercise is a great precursor or addendum to exploring your actual results on the online Love Talk Indicator. If you have them handy, see how your perceptions lined up with reality—for both yourself and your partner. This is sure to generate a helpful discussion and raise your awareness level of your two talk styles.

THE HEAD/HEART SELF-TEST

Below are a number of pairs of personal characteristics or traits. For each pair, choose the trait that describes you more. Mark A if you are more "imaginative," or B if you value being "rational." Some of the traits will appear twice, but always in combination with a different trait. There are no right or wrong answers. Please be honest.

Choose the word in each pair that best completes this sentence for you:

I am more . . .

1. A. imaginative   B. rational
2. A. helpful   B. quick-witted
3. A. neat   B. sympathetic
4. A. level-headed   B. efficient
5. A. intelligent   B. considerate
6. A. self-reliant   B. ambitious
7. A. respectful   B. original
8. A. creative   B. sensible
9. A. generous   B. individualistic
10. A. responsible   B. original
11. A. capable   B. tolerant
12. A. trustworthy   B. wise
13. A. neat   B. logical
14. A. forgiving   B. gentle
15. A. efficient   B. respectful
16. A. alert   B. cooperative

17.   A. imaginative   B. helpful
18.   A. realistic   B. moral
19.   A. considerate   B. wise
20.   A. sympathetic   B. individualistic
21.   A. ambitious   B. patient

Now take a moment to score the first part of this questionnaire. Give yourself a point for each answer that matches the following key. Note that numbers 1, 4, 6, 8, 10, and 13 are buffers and are not used in the scoring.

2. a _____   15. b _____
3. b _____   16. b _____
5. b _____   17. a _____
7. a _____   18. b _____
9. a _____   19. a _____
11. b _____   20. a _____
12. a _____   21. b _____
14. a _____

                     Total: _____

Now answer each of the following items by placing a number beside each of the items as follows:

1 Rarely or none of the time   4 A good part of the time
2 A little of the time   5 Most or all of the time
3 Some of the time

_____ When my partner and I have a disagreement, I win.

_____ I'm more hard-driving than my partner.

_____ I'm very good at solving problems for my partner.

_____ Compared to my partner, I keep my feelings in check.

_____ I'm good at accurately analyzing a situation or issue in our marriage.

_____ I'm a natural problem solver.

_____ Compared to my partner, I confront conflict head-on.

_____ I'm assertive.

_____ Relative to my partner, I'm more goal-oriented.

_____ I like to get to the facts more than my partner.

_____ I have more "rules" about doing things than my partner.

_____ I feel my partner is emotional.

_____ I take control more than my partner does.

_____ Compared to my partner, I would rather zero in on a solution than explore feelings.

_____ I'm less sentimental than my partner.

_____ I'm not easy to please because my expectations are high.

_____ Compared to my partner, I'm more likely to criticize and pressure people to get things done.

_____ I have no problem making my own needs known.

_____ Compared to my partner, I'm less likely to show my emotions.

_____ I want to be in control more than my partner does.

Score this self-test by totaling up your points on the items. There is a potential score of 20 to 100.

Total _____

The two parts of this questionnaire give you two subscores. The first half of the test reveals your heart score, while the second half reveals your head score. Note them here:

Your heart score: _____

Your head score: _____

Making Sense of Your Head/Heart Self-Test

There are 15 possible points on the Heart Talk Test (indicating where you are in your inclination to sympathize). If you scored 7 points or more, you are probably in the "high heart" zone. Below 7 points puts you in the "low heart" zone. Note your heart score on this continuum.

Low Heart Talk   High Heart Talk

1   7   15

There are 100 points on the Head Talk Test (indicating where you are in your inclination to analyze). If you scored 50 or higher on this test, you are probably in the "high head" zone. Below 50 points puts you in the "low head" zone. Note your head score on this continuum.

Low Head Talk   High Head Talk

1   7   15

As we've said in the book, some people talk with their heart but not their head; they tend to sympathize more than analyze. Others analyze more than sympathize. You now know which camp you tend to fall into.

Are both of your scores high? Congratulations! You've learned to balance your head talk and heart talk. You've probably worked at this and are adept at using both when trying to make a meaningful connection with your partner. You sympathize as well as analyze. In other words, you *empathize.* You possess the precious secret to emotional connection. You hold an invaluable tool for any couple wanting to enjoy Love Talk: empathy.

Now perhaps you scored low on both Head Talk and Heart Talk; you neither sympathize nor analyze. That's okay. This simply means you presently tend to *personalize* more than empathize. In other words, for a number of possible reasons, you currently have a tough time seeing beyond your own boundaries. Chances are you're carrying some emotional pain. Perhaps you've been burned in a previous relationship and, like the turtle retreating into its shell, you currently withdraw in order to feel safe, to not get burned again. It's only natural and you shouldn't feel guilty for being in this place. With time and effort, as well as patience from your partner, you'll soon move beyond it.

Now let's get something clear before we go any further: if you or your partner's scores don't happen to land you in the territory of empathy—if you or your partner tend to sympathize but not analyze or vice versa, or if you or your partner tend to do neither—don't feel badly, not even for a minute. You're not alone. The vast majority of couples are in the same boat. That's why communication is consistently ranked as the number one frustration across the board for couples.[1] More important, every couple, no matter their age or stage, can move into Love Talk with a few pointers and some intentional effort. As you will soon see, it generally requires only a tune-up, not an overhaul.

---

[1]Wayne Rickerson, "Just Us," *Virtue* (July/August 1984), 44.

THE EMPATHY EXERCISE

We're glad you are using the workbook exercise for this chapter.
You'll get much more out of this exercise than simply hearing or
reading about it. So here we go.

First, close your eyes and see yourself, in your mind's eye, as your
partner. Do your best to imagine what it would be like to be living in her
skin. Take a good sixty seconds to ponder this.

Next, consider a typical day and ask yourself the following questions.
We've provided space under each one for you to jot notes so you can later
compare your thoughts with your partner's.

On a typical day as your partner . . .

1. What time would you get up in the morning and how did
   you sleep? What would your morning mood like and why?

2. How long would it take you to get ready for the day? Would
   you spend more or less time in front of the mirror? What
   would you wear?

3. When would you leave the house, if you left at all? What
   would your activities through the day be?

4. What would you worry about in a typical day? What would be your likely stress points?

5. What would bring you the greatest joy or satisfaction during a typical day?

6. Would you have different financial responsibilities or pressures?

7. Would you eat differently? Exercise? Would you be more or less concerned about your physical appearance?

8. Would you feel more or less self-assured?

9. How would you feel toward the end of the day as you're getting ready for dinner? What would be on your mind?

10. And how would you feel about your partner (that would be you!)? What would you want most from your partner? How would you communicate with your partner?

Congratulations on completing these questions. You undoubtedly have a unique and fresh perspective on life in your partner's skin after doing this. Now take a few minutes to review your experience with your partner. Compare notes and invite feedback on your take of life as your partner.

SPEAKING HER LANGUAGE

W e'll say it again: men analyze while women sympathize. Relative to men, women are focused on the here and now. While you are analyzing plans and solving problems for a better tomorrow, she is focused on what's going on right now between the two of you. Why does this matter? Because you can save yourself countless hours of frustration by learning to pay a little less attention to the "report" (and how it impacts your plans) and a little more to your "rapport" (and how it impacts your present relationship with her). Here's how:

First, rate how much you want—truly desire—to build rapport with your partner. How much do you really want to have conversations that bring you closer together? Be honest. Use this scale to make it concrete.

No Desire   Intense Desire

1   2   3   4   5   6   7   8   9   10

This simple rating is important because it forces you to own up to what may be your biggest obstacle in crossing the communication gender line. If you truly have little desire to connect with your partner (if you are ranking it at 4 or lower), you probably have much more going on than simple gender differences. You may feel wounded or deeply misunderstood, or you may even have a biological issue that requires medical help. On average, most men in a typical relationship rank this desire at about 7. Most men want to build rapport with their woman, but it isn't necessarily their highest felt need.

Give yourself a few minutes to reflect on each of the following items.

Since building rapport may not be a natural inclination for you, you've got to become aware of the times you are least likely to have the ability to lean into rapport talk. So begin by tapping into the times you are most task-oriented. When are you most likely to be goal-focused? Maybe it's when you are paying the bills. Perhaps it's in the first hour after you get home from work and want to read your mail or the paper. You understand. When are those times you are most task-oriented at home? Note a couple of them here:

1. _____
2. _____

Now do your best to identify the times when your partner is most likely to want to build rapport. When does she most want to connect with you? Maybe it's the minute you get home from work. Perhaps it's right after dinner or just before you go to bed. Note a couple of those times when she is most predictably interested in building rapport:

1. _____
2. _____

Next, identify the biggest stumbling blocks you have to personally focusing on the here and now with your partner. Undoubtedly, it's going to be when you are most task-oriented, but it may also be when you are especially hungry, or when you are catching up on email, or when you are watching a game on television. Note a couple of those times:

1. _____
2. _____

Now you have the raw materials to work with. Now you know your danger zones—those times and places you and your partner are most likely to clash in your conversations. All you need to do now is locate the best times and places for you to invest in building rapport with your partner. In other words, at what point in your day are you most likely to patiently ask questions and listen—and don't say after she goes to sleep! Even if this is not your highest priority, we want you to identify when you are *most* up for it. Give this some serious thought and clue your partner in. The most important aspect of this exercise involves talking with her about it. She has done a similar reflection in her workbook, so set aside a few minutes over a cup of coffee to delve into this one.

Do You Hear
What She Hears?

It's not so much what your partner is saying to you; it's what you *hear* your partner saying to you. That's why reflecting her feelings is one of the most helpful and difficult listening techniques to implement. Following are some statements your partner might make. Read each separately, listening for feelings beneath the words. Make note of the feelings you hear and write out a response that reflects that feeling for each of the statements (see examples). We're giving you just five of these to try, so it won't take long to do.

Examples:

Statement: "Just once I'd like not to have to pick your coat off this chair."

Reflection of feeling: "That has to be aggravating, I know. I'll do my best to hang up my coat in the closet."

Statement: "I can't believe you agreed to do this tonight without asking me first."

Reflection of feeling: "Sounds like you are feeling upset."

1. "I don't want your advice!"

   _____

2. "Wendy used to email or phone me, but I haven't heard from her in ages."

_____

3. "You need to call me if you're running late so I know what's going on."

_____

4. "I'm not sure what to do about my manager at work. He's so unreasonable with his deadlines."

_____

5. "There is no way I'm going to let my mother spoil this party by rearranging the seats at the table this year."

_____

Now compare your list of reflective statements to those listed below to see how accurately you recognized the possible feelings. Give yourself a 2 on those items your choice closely matches, a 1 on items your choice only partially matches, and a 0 if you missed altogether.

Possible responses:

1. "Sounds like you'd just like to be understood."
2. "You must feel hurt by that."
3. "That must be frustrating—I need to do that for you."
4. "Sounds like you're really feeling pressured at work."
5. "You sound pretty determined to set your boundaries."

Score _____

How you rate on listening for feelings beneath the words:

8–10   Above average recognition of feelings

5–7   Average recognition of feelings

0–4   Below average recognition of feelings

READING YOUR PARTNER'S BODY LANGUAGE

Can you accurately read the face of your partner? Do you speak her body language? Complete the quiz below to find out how well you listen with the third ear. Record your answers at left, by marking either Y (yes), S/M (sometimes/maybe), or N (no) for each question. Add up your scores according to the instructions below, and then read the information that follows to learn how you can improve your ability to read others.

_____ Do you know that there are certain days of the week that are best to approach your partner with a new idea or a favor to ask?

_____ Have you had run-ins or difficulties getting along with your partner over the same issues again and again because you "just don't understand"?*

_____ At a dinner party with several people, have you ever thought you would get the attention of your partner by doing or saying something she would like, but then you discover that she barely noticed?*

_____ When you are having problems with a friend or a colleague at work and you talk to your partner about it, do you already know the kind of response she will give you?

_____ When your partner retreats to a part of the house without telling you what she's up to, do you know when to let her unwind alone and when to ask questions?

_____ When you are enjoying a romantic moment with sweet kisses, are you able to quickly tell if she has something more in mind than just kissing?

_____ When you ask your partner if she likes what you are wearing and she says she does, are you ever surprised to learn later that she really doesn't like it but didn't want to hurt your feelings?*

_____ Do you and your partner have a way of communicating non-verbally at a party when you can't use words in front of other people?

_____ When your partner asks for advice on something that's troubling her, are you quick to give her several suggestions to make the situation better?*

_____ Your partner is doodling on a paper napkin while the two of you are discussing something that's troubling her. Do you immediately know what her doodling is about (what it says about her feelings)?

_____ You leave a message for your partner to call you on your cell phone as soon as she can. You carry it with you all day and never get her call. Do you assume she is especially busy?

_____ In a discussion, your partner keeps glancing up and to the right while she is thinking of a response to your questions. Do you know what this means?

Scoring

If the question is marked with this symbol (*), the scoring is as follows: Y = 4, S/M = 2, N = 0. If the question isn't marked, the scoring is as follows: Y = 0, S/M = 2, N = 4.

Making Sense of Your Score and Learning More

Any score over 24 means you read your partner well, but you could probably benefit from a brief brushup on these strategies that ensure that you have an edge.

- Learn your partner's body language. For example, when she leans forward to talk, it shows a letting down of her guard. When she clasps her hands behind her back, it reveals frustration. When her palms are open, so is she. When she sits with her hands clasped behind her head, it means "you'd better impress me."

- Know when your partner is nervous. Here's what to look for: clearing the throat, running tongue along front teeth, twiddling thumbs, fidgeting with a watch or bracelet, wearing a tight lipped grin, and shifting the eyes. Any or all of these will be present when your partner is feeling put on the spot or otherwise anxious.

- Read your partner's silence. If you're making a proposal for your idea of a perfect vacation and your partner shows little reaction, she may be distracted or annoyed. But if she is making eye contact with you and leaning forward, your message is getting through.

- Focus on her face. More than anyone in your life, your sweetheart's moods are revealed in subtle facial expressions. The raising of one eyebrow means she has questions. An upturned corner of one side of her mouth says she's frustrated or cynical. Biting her bottom lip means she is sincere. And blinking more than usual means she may not be telling the truth.

- Pinpoint her big needs. A key to reading anyone in a romantic relationship is to know her top ten needs and how they are expressed. If solitude is one of her big needs, for example, she may fold her arms and look to the floor when she needs time alone. If she needs affirmation, her eyes will widen. If she needs recreation and activity, she may bounce her leg while sitting in a chair to signal boredom. So explore her big needs to read her little cues.

- Get a read on your partner's anxiety level. She may say she's made a decision she feels good about, but if she is chewing a pen, biting her fingernails, or pinching her flesh, you can bet she's not feeling confident. If she was self-assured, she'd be sitting up straight in her chair with her hands comfortably folded in her lap or together in a "steepled" position with her elbows on the chair's arms.

- Look for solutions when you get stumped. If you are continually getting mixed signals from your partner's body language, don't blame her. Work to understand what is really going on and be creative in finding avenues to better understand her. She may have some unique body language quirks that you can understand only after you know what they mean.

I WANT TO READ
YOUR MIND

We often practice this technique. When it comes to halting a misperception in its tracks, this quick strategy can work wonders, and we want to give you a chance right now to see just what we mean.

Take a moment to consider a topic currently affecting you and your partner. It may have to do with how much time you spend working, how you manage money, your spiritual life, your hobbies. Anything at all. Simply consider some loose end currently on the table (at least from your perspective) between the two of you, and take a moment to write down exactly what you think she is saying to herself about it.

By the way, be sure to choose a topic about which you don't know for sure what she is thinking (she hasn't come right out and said anything directly about it), but you have your hunches because of some subtle hints you have picked up on.

For example, you may be thinking she is upset with the amount of time you spend talking on your cell phone because you thought you saw her roll her eyes the last time you took a call when you were on a date together. If that's the issue for you, you might write something like: "I wish he would never use that thing when he is around me." You get the idea. Write what you think she is saying to herself about whatever issue you choose:

Issue:

Her self-talk about it:

_____

Now, read what you wrote about this to your partner and ask her to rate how accurate it is on the following scale:

    Not Accurate   Right on the Nose

Try another one if you like . . .

Issue:

Her self-talk about it:

_____

Now read what you wrote about this to your partner and ask her to rate how accurate it is on the following scale:

    Not Accurate   Right on the Nose

1   2   3   4   5   6   7   8   9   10

See how it works? Now you know just how well you are reading her mind on this hunch you've been harboring. You can use this technique anytime you catch yourself making assumptions about what she is thinking or feeling. Sometimes you may be right; sometimes you may be wrong. It doesn't matter. The important thing is that this quick technique helps you easily zero in on the facts—on reality. Then you know for sure what you are dealing with.

Make this kind of "mind reading" a habit and you'll keep unnecessary misunderstanding at bay.

Is It Time to Clam Up?

Sometimes the best way to have a conversation is simply to stop talking about something. The key is knowing what those somethings are. Consider each of the following scenarios and determine which of them are issues to talk about or issues to clam up about. We provide you with three options under each one. Be honest in giving your opinion about what you would do in that situation.

1. Your partner is dying to delve into what you are thinking about a potential job change, but you aren't quite ready to talk about it because you know it's going to be intense. What do you do?

    A. Talk about it anyway.
    B. Say: "Honestly, I don't know when I'll ever be ready to get into that conversation with you."
    C. Say: "I need some more time to think about this, but I will be ready to talk after dinner tonight."

2. You and your partner have had the same conversation a million times about whether to drive a used car and be debt-free or buy a brand-new vehicle and carry debt. After countless attempts to find common ground, you know you're highly unlikely to see eye to eye on it anytime soon. So when she brings it up again, you are most likely to:

    A. Rationally try one more time to make your case and convince her to agree with you.

    B.   Get emotional and say how blatantly wrong she is to believe that way.

    C.   Refuse to talk about it, to even mention it, for at least a month.

3. You are trying to decide with your partner whether to attend a party that you know will be boring but will likely be an opportunity to network with people who can open up some doors for you. You're exhausted and don't want to go. Suddenly, your partner goes into a tirade and gets overly emotional—even irrational—saying that you are lazy and that it would be unthinkable not to attend. You are most likely to:

    A.   Come back with equal emotion about how unthinkable it is for her to put this kind of pressure on you.

    B.   Say: "Do you have any idea how ridiculous you sound right now?"

    C.   Say: "I'm going to give you some space for a few minutes and then we can talk after you pull it together."

4. Your partner is driving home from work and phones you on her cell to tell you that she was given a huge project that may eat up some of your weekend. You are likely to:

    A.   Sulk and whine a bit about missing out on some fun stuff you had hoped to do during your weekend together.

    B.   Say: "I guess I don't have any say in that." And clam up.

    C.   Say: "I know you didn't ask for my advice, but can I offer a suggestion about how you can get your project done earlier so we can still salvage our weekend?"

Okay, let's see how you fared. There's no scoring to be done here. This is an exercise to simply get your wheels turning on when and how to halt a conversation when needed. In each of these scenarios, we propose that the best answer is C, since this category of answers helps you put on the brakes in a situation that is otherwise likely to run amuck.

ENOUGH ADVICE ALREADY!

The true secret of giving advice," said Hannah Whitall Smith, "is to be perfectly indifferent whether it is taken or not, and never persist in trying to set people right." Don't you agree? Of course! Who wouldn't? But we don't know of anyone who would say it is easy to put this wisdom into practice. Advice sometimes comes from a genuine effort to help and sometimes from a more devious motive to hurt, as in, "You'd have more friends if you weren't so conceited." In other words, advice tends to fall along a continuum—and it's received or heard along a continuum as well.

That's why we want you to begin this exercise by rating where you tend to fall along these two scales:

Are you . . .

Open to advice   Resistant to advice

-5   -4   -3   -2   -1   0   1   2   3   4   5

Open to critique   Resistant to critique

-5   -4   -3   -2   -1   0   1   2   3   4   5

Why do you rate yourself the way you do on these two scales? In other words, on what do you base your judgment?

_____

_____

If your ratings are different on each of the above scales, why? In other words, how do you distinguish advice and critique?

_____

_____

Now we ask you to do the same rating for your partner. On these two scales, where do you perceive her to fall?

Your partner is . . .

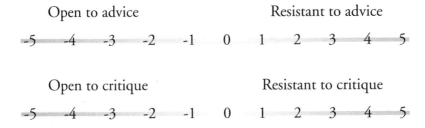

Open to advice   Resistant to advice

-5   -4   -3   -2   -1   0   1   2   3   4   5

Open to critique   Resistant to critique

-5   -4   -3   -2   -1   0   1   2   3   4   5

Okay, now here's the tricky part. Your partner has done the same thing in her workbook (want to now reconsider your answers?). So to help you get this issue out on the table and have a positive discussion (the kind characterized by Love Talk) about advice-giving and criticism in your relationship, we want you to compare notes.

We realize, of course, that this can be a touchy subject. That's why we urge you not to do this if either of you is in a bad mood. This discussion requires a calm mind and an unselfish heart. Its sole purpose is to help you talk about advice-giving so you better understand each other. In other words, it's to help facilitate a deeper level of empathy.

So whether it's now or later, take a deep breath, lower your defenses, center your thoughts, and put yourself in your partner's shoes as you talk about giving and receiving advice and critique. And keep the wisdom of Hannah Whitall Smith in mind: give up trying to set your partner straight.

TUNING IN TO
YOUR SELF-TALK

You've probably heard the old adage, "There's nothing wrong with talking to yourself. But when you start answering back, it's time to worry." Whoever came up with this quip was wrong. Talking aloud to yourself in public isn't a sign of positive mental health, but holding an internal dialogue is not only normal, but useful. Your inner conversations have a powerful impact on your emotional well-being and, of course, your relationships. Becoming aware of exactly what you are saying *to* yourself *about* yourself can help you understand why you react the way you do to events and people in your life. It can help you figure out who you are, control your moods, repeat your successes, and short-circuit your shortcomings.

The key, of course, is to uncover exactly what you are saying when you talk to yourself. The following is a quick self-talk test that will help you zero in on your internal dialogue. Take as much time as you need to honestly answer these ten questions. When you are finished, we'll help you identify your self-talk style.

1. You are hosting a dinner party and everything goes well until the dessert, when you realize you forgot to pick up the pastry shells for the ice cream. At the end of the evening, you are most likely say to yourself:

    A. Who cares? The evening was a great success.

    B. Sure, the dinner party went all right, but dessert was a failure.

    C. I ruined everything when I didn't remember to go to the bakery.

2. You have a project at work that requires your team's support and you are very eager and excited to get moving on it. At a meeting, however, one of your colleagues raises numerous questions about your idea and suggests you hold off until the team has more time to think about it. You most likely say to yourself:

    A. He might have a good point.

    B. He doesn't trust me.

    C. He is either for me or against me.

3. The words that most aptly describe your internal dialogue about yourself are:

    A. Positive and upbeat.

    B. Neutral and on the fence.

    C. Negative and critical.

4. You've just made a major mistake at work that potentially cost the company a major sale. What are you most likely to say to yourself in the next day or two?

    A. I may have made a mistake, but I'm still a worthwhile person.

    B. I never measure up to the person I want to be.

    C. I'm worthless.

5. You enjoy a much-needed outing with friends. When you arrive home, you find your spouse sprawled on the couch, watching television, and leftover pizza and stacks of dirty plates and cups on the kitchen counter. You most likely say to yourself:

A. My spouse must be exhausted. I'll whip those dishes into shape and then relax on the couch too.

B. I never get to go out by myself. Couldn't my partner at least be courteous enough to clean up this one time?

C. I never should have gone out. Things completely fall apart when I'm gone.

6. When you were a kid, what kind of messages did you most often receive from your parents?

A. Encouraging and loving messages.

B. An equal amount of encouraging and critical messages.

C. Critical and hurtful messages.

7. You are headed out for the evening and want to wear one of your favorite shirts. It is just finishing the final cycle in your washing machine. You put it in the dryer and the dryer shorts out. It's completely dead, no power. And your shirt is completely wet. You realize it won't be dry in time to wear it. You most likely say to yourself:

A. No problem, I'll wear something else.

B. It never fails. This always happens to me.

C. I can't stand this. My whole evening is ruined.

8. You need a helping hand to move some heavy furniture and wonder about asking a friend. What thought is most likely to shoot through your brain?

A. I'm pretty sure he can help, and if not, he'll say so.

B. Am I pushing the limits of this friendship too far?

C. I don't deserve to have anyone help me, so I'd better not even ask.

9. Your tennis opponent says out loud to himself, "What a lousy shot!" What are you most likely to do?

A. Say, "You're being too hard on yourself."

B. Remain silent.

C. Say, "You're right; I've seen better."

10. In general, the internal conversation you have with yourself most days tends to:

A. Help you experience more fully and consistently your profound significance.

B. Go back and forth between helping and hindering your experience of profound significance.

C. Keep you from experiencing your profound significance.

Scoring

If you answered mainly A, it's safe to say that your self-talk is based on a solid sense of significance. You tend to consistently see things in their proper perspective and rarely punish yourself for mistakes. Your self-talk is based on the reality of the situation. If your shirt was wet, for example, you would simply choose another shirt. No big deal. Also, your negative situations don't tend to elicit a negative emotional response. This is a sure sign of well-schooled self-talk. Plus, if you've made a mistake, you don't see yourself as a mistake—a sure sign of profound significance. In general, you are secure in yourself and enjoy a depth of self-worth. You have learned to use your self-talk as a tool to maintain your dignity and significance. Of course, if nearly every one of your answers was A, you may want to review how honest you are being with yourself. Rarely does a person answer every item like this.

If you answered mainly B, your self-talk tends to be more negative than is beneficial. While you are not likely to punish yourself for very long with a condemning internal dialogue, you certainly are not using your self-talk to maximize your experience of profound significance. You are literally talking yourself out of the full enjoyment of being loved at your core. There is much you can learn to improve your self-talk.

If you answered mainly C, your self-talk shows signs of needing serious attention and repair. In all likelihood, you are suffering from a low sense of self-worth and your self-talk is keeping at bay any chance of experiencing abiding and positive self-worth. Almost reflexively, you immediately equate any failure or bad experience to your own "badness." You have a very difficult time separating who you are from what you do. No doubt, you already know your internal dialogue is repeatedly sabotaging your ability to appreciate your significance and worth. What can you do? Plenty. This section of *Love Talk* will help you improve your self-talk, but you also may want to consider a few sessions with a life-coach or a counselor who can provide you with help specifically for you.

Are the results of a self-test like this generalizations? Of course. Since we aren't meeting with you one-on-one, face-to-face, we don't have the luxury of examining unique nuances and subtleties of how your use or abuse yourself through internal dialogue. However, this simple self-test can at least help you identify your general tendencies so you personalize the content of this part of *Love Talk*.

TESTING YOUR
RESPECT LEVELS

Take a moment to answer the dozen true and false questions below. They will give you a quick idea where you stand on respecting yourself and your partner. Take your time and be honest in your answers.

1. I honor my partner's decisions.

   Rarely   Much of the Time   Always

   1   2   3   4   5   6   7   8   9   10

2. I feel proud to be with my partner.

   Rarely   Much of the Time   Always

   1   2   3   4   5   6   7   8   9   10

3. I believe our relationship is great because of my partner.

   Rarely   Much of the Time   Always

   1   2   3   4   5   6   7   8   9   10

4. I sincerely appreciate what my partner brings to our relationship.

   Rarely   Much of the Time   Always

   1   2   3   4   5   6   7   8   9   10

5. I feel very secure in my partner's commitment to me.

   Rarely   Much of the Time   Always

   1   2   3   4   5   6   7   8   9   10

6. I really prize how special my partner is.

   Rarely   Much of the Time   Always

   1   2   3   4   5   6   7   8   9   10

7. I believe I am doing the very best I can as a partner.

   Rarely   Much of the Time   Always

   1   2   3   4   5   6   7   8   9   10

8. I know I'm deeply loved by my partner.

   Rarely   Much of the Time   Always

   1   2   3   4   5   6   7   8   9   10

9. I make sure my own needs (as well as my partner's) get met.

   Rarely   Much of the Time   Always

   1   2   3   4   5   6   7   8   9   10

10. I have confidence in my ability to make good decisions.

    Rarely   Much of the Time   Always

    1   2   3   4   5   6   7   8   9   10

11. I know I'm still worthwhile even when I disappoint my partner.

    Rarely   Much of the Time   Always

    1   2   3   4   5   6   7   8   9   10

12. I'm not afraid to speak my mind, and I don't sweep my feelings under the rug.

    Rarely   Much of the Time   Always

    1   2   3   4   5   6   7   8   9   10

Scoring

Add up your score for items 1 through 6. This is your partner-respect score.

Next, tally your answers for items 7 through 12. This is your self-respect score.

Partner-respect score: _____

Self-respect score: _____

Talking from Your Strengths

You read in the book how valuable this exercise can be for both of you. So let's jump right into it. Consider some specific remarks that would give a good boost to your partner's self-esteem in each of these areas noted in the Strengths Chart on the following page. Take time to seriously ponder each one.

Once you have completed this chart, we guarantee that your partner would love to see it—and hear you walk her through it. In fact, this is crucial to improving your mutual respect. So take some time as a couple to share what you wrote on your charts. You may find that this is the most enjoyable exercise in this workbook.

One more thing. As you hear your spouse recount her list of admirable qualities about you, don't feel compelled to comment. And certainly don't discount them (this will be a temptation if you are low on self-respect). This is time to simply soak it in. Enjoy!

THE STRENGTHS CHART		
	My Spouse's Strengths	Specific Example of the Trait
Mental 1. 2.		
Social 1. 2.		
Physical 1. 2.		
Spiritual 1. 2.		

FOR SMALL GROUP
DISCUSSION WITH THE
DVD CURRICULUM

Studying this material in a small group with other couples is one of the best ways to make it stick—and have a lot of fun in the process. Each session will feature a video component featuring Les and Leslie Parrott as well as other creative elements.

After viewing the video, you will find discussion questions on the following pages that you can use in each of your six small group sessions under the section "Talking about Talking." Don't get hung up on answering every one of them in order. Use the questions that work best for the personality of your group.

You will see that some of the sessions are based on more than one chapter from the book *Love Talk*. You'll also discover that not all chapters in the book are covered in these sessions since most groups feel that six sessions is just about the right length for a small group series. Of course, you can always feel free to bring into your group discussions any of the content you'd like to explore from the book chapters that are not highlighted in your six sessions.

Obviously, you are going to get more out of the discussion if you've read the pertinent chapters. But if you haven't read the book, don't worry. You can still join the discussion and you don't need to feel an ounce of guilt. The purpose is to enjoy the interaction and learn from it. You can read the book at a later date if you wish.

You'll also find that each of the sessions will rely on an exercise or two from this workbook under the heading "Talking through Your Workbook Exercises." We've selected exercises that will not put anyone on the spot or force anyone to share information they don't want to. Of course, your group may elect to use other exercises from this workbook to discuss. It's up to you and your group.

A key ingredient to successful small group discussion is vulnerability. Typically, the more transparent you are, the more meaningful the experience will be. And the more open others will be as well. Vulnerability begets vulnerability. However, we caution you not to use this time to gripe about your partner in some way. Don't embarrass each other by dragging out dirty laundry you know would upset your partner. Of course, this can cause each of you to walk a narrow line. You want to be genuine and vulnerable, but not at the expense of your partner's feelings.

Another key ingredient in these discussions is specificity. You'll gain much more out of this time when you use specific examples with each other. So with this in mind, we will remind you to be specific every so often.

If you have the time, there is also a section called "Talking Together as a Couple" that both of you can do in between small group sessions. These exercises are found in this workbook and will help you discover other ways you can encourage each other to become better at Love Talk.

One more thing: Each session begins with a question that is "just for fun"—a kind of icebreaker. We've selected one question from our accompanying book *Love Talk Starters,* which contains 275 similar kinds of questions. They are just to get the wheels turning as you come together as a group. You can order this little book of fun questions at www.Real Relationships.com.

So relax. Have fun. And learn all you can to enjoy more Love Talk.

Session One

COMMUNICATION 101

(Based on chapters 2 and 3 in Love Talk*)*

Just for Fun (5 minutes)

If you were your partner's publicist, what would you want the media to know about her? And what show would you like to see her be a guest on?

Video Notes (10–15 minutes)

Talking about Talking (30 minutes)

1. Do you agree that communication is the "lifeblood" of your relationship? Why or why not?

   And if so, in what specific ways has your communication nourished your bond together in the past seven days? Be specific.

2. When do the two of you tend to have your best conversations together? In other words, what are the ingredients that go into a great conversation for you as a couple?

3. What's one practical thing you can do this coming week to ensure you have a meaningful time to connect?

4. When it comes to brushing up on the basics of communication, which item do you need to work on most?

   • Carving out time in your schedule to talk on purpose
   • Attending to your partner's message with your body language
   • Listening to the feelings underneath your partner's words
   • Clarifying the content of your partner's messages
   • Steering clear of unwanted advice

Select the one you need to work on most and talk to the group about why you selected it and then identify one specific action you can take in the next twenty-four hours to improve on it.

Talking through Your Workbook Exercises (10 minutes)

Within your small group, take time to complete Exercise 1 in your workbook. This exercise asks you to explore your communication goals as individuals and as a couple. If you feel comfortable, share what you learned about yourself and your relationship from doing this exercise with the rest of the group. What are the specific goals you came up with? Are they similar to other people's goals in your group?

Talking Together as a Couple

Spend some time this week as a couple completing Exercise 3 in this workbook, which asks you to identify your current communication strengths as a couple. About twenty potential strengths are noted in the list from this exercise. What is your top one or two as a couple? In other words, which one of these strengths do you two share in common that tops your list of communication strengths and why? Use an example to back up your opinion.

Chapter 2 in the book *Love Talk* explains that "talking techniques" can fall short when we are not genuinely interested in what our partner has to say. In other words, they fail when we are simply going through the motions. When are you most likely to not be fully present and genuine with your partner? It may be when you are hungry, working on a task, just getting home from work, and so forth. You get the idea. Be specific and feel free to refer to Exercise 4 in this workbook as well.

Session Two

THE FOUNDATION OF EVERY GREAT CONVERSATION

(Based on chapter 4 in Love Talk*)*

Just for Fun (5 minutes)

What would the two of you do with a free Saturday and $1000 that had to be spent that day?

Video Notes (10–15 minutes)

Talking about Talking (30 minutes)

1. Do you agree that the greatest stumbling block to speaking each other's language is your personal fear factor, your feeling unsafe with your partner because your primary safety need is being threatened? Why or why not?

2. Imagine a physical space in your home that would be known as the "safe room." It would be a room where you could have confidence in knowing you would never be threatened with the fear of losing your emotional safety needs. How and when would you use it? What conversation topics would you reserve for that space?

3. Identify the other individuals in your group that share your emotional fear factor (time, approval, loyalty, or quality). Take a minute or two in these small subgroups to note what you want others to know about your fear factor and then come back together and take turns sharing this with the group.

4. What is your least important fear factor? What fear factor matters most to you? Share this with the group and ask for input from others who identify this fear factor as their most important one? Ask them to help you understand why that fear factor matters so much to them.

5. Knowing each other's perceived fear factors, how might you approach your conversations differently? In other words, how might you use this information to improve them?

Talking through Your Workbook Exercises (10 minutes)

Within your small group, take time to complete Exercise 8 in your workbook, which asks you to identify your personal fear factor. Discuss with the group what you learned about your emotional safety needs from this exercise. Do you and your partner agree on which of the four safety needs tops your list? Why or why not? Next, share with the group what you learned about each other's top emotional security needs that you didn't know before this exercise.

Talking Together as a Couple

Spend some time this week as a couple completing Exercise 5 in this workbook. This asks you to assess how you spend your time in an average week in order to discover how you can find time to talk together as a couple. If you can find more time together, what can you do? What kind of time together do you consider "quality" time? Use an example to back up your opinion.

Session Three

YOUR PERSONAL TALK STYLE

(Based on chapters 5–9 in Love Talk*)*

Just for Fun (5 minutes)

What did the two of you do on your very first date, and what was your impression of each other?

Video Notes (10–15 minutes)

Talking about Talking (30 minutes)

1. Which one of you would be considered the more aggressive problem solver and why? In your group, divide into two sub-groups—aggressive problem solvers and passive problem solvers. Take a moment in your subgroups to note what you think the other group needs to know about you and why?

2. Identify a recent time when you tried to influence your partner. It may have been about something major or minor. It could have been on anything from what restaurant to eat at, to what to wear, to how generous to be. In this situation, were you influencing more with facts or feelings? Which one is more important to you (in other words, which one impacts you more) and why?

3. What's the biggest change the two of you have had to face in the past year, be it positive or negative? How did you each adjust and cope with the change? How would you describe your differing or similar styles?

4. Identify a decision the two of you had to make together. Something that stands out in your memory bank. Which one of you was more cautious? More spontaneous? Or are you both the

same? Is this representative of most decisions you make together? Why or why not?

Talking through Your Workbook Exercises (10 minutes)

Within your small group, take time to complete Exercise 9 in your workbook. This will help you identify your personal talk style. Share what you learned about your style with the group.

Talking Together as a Couple

If you would like to explore your talk style at a much more accurate and helpful level, take the online Love Talk Indicator at www.RealRela tionships.com to receive your personal talk style report. While this report does cost money, it may allow you to understand your Love Talk style at a much deeper level and the investment may pay great dividends in your relationship. Share your results with each other and then bring your profile to the group and share what you found most helpful and insightful from it. Of course, in this setting, seek to learn not only about yourself, but about others that are sharing their results as well.

Session Four

THE SECRET TO EMOTIONAL CONNECTION

(Based on chapter 10 in Love Talk*)*

Just for Fun (5 minutes)

Have you studied your partner's funny bone? What's one thing you can always say or do to get a laugh out of your partner?

Video Notes (10–15 minutes)

Talking about Talking (30 minutes)

1. If you are like most people the thought of having your positive and negative comments toward your partner tabulated is a scary one. But if you can muster up courage, bravely share with the group what percentage you would have in each category if the results were based on the last forty-eight hours.

2. Your partner brings home a problem. Which are you more likely to do: analyze or sympathize? Why do you believe this is so? Does your partner agree with you? Consider a recent example of how you are more prone to analyze or sympathize and share it with the group.

3. Think of a time in your life when you changed your perspective after seeing a situation from another person's point of view. This does not have to involve your partner. Share that experience with the group and reveal what you learned about yourself from it. What does it tell you about the power of empathy?

4. Empathy is a primary tool for tapping into your partner's top emotional safety need. Share with the group how you plan to specifically empathize with your partner. How will you use your head and your heart to better understand her emotional fear

factor? Be practical and specific. And what difference do you think your empathy with your partner in this way will make in your relationship?

Talking through Your Workbook Exercises (10 minutes)

Within your small group, take time to complete Exercise 10 in your workbook. This exercise provides a self-test to help you determine if you are more likely to use your head or your heart. What do you think of your results? What new light did this exercise shed for you? What can you do personally to empathize with your head and heart better with your partner? Be specific.

Talking Together as a Couple

Exercise 11 in your workbook calls on you to enter the world of your partner. What parts were easy and which ones were difficult for you? What did you learn about your partner and yourself in doing this empathy exercise? Next time you meet with your group, relay to them what this exercise was like for you.

Session Five

WHEN NOT TO TALK

(Based on chapter 13 in Love Talk*)*

Just for Fun (5 minutes)

If you could have any singer or musical group perform at your partner's next birthday party, who would it be and what song would you have them sing?

Video Notes (10–15 minutes)

Talking about Talking (30 minutes)

1. What was your first reaction to this session's title and topic? Are you surprised to find a session that tells you to quit talking to each other? Do you agree that there are specific times when this is the best thing to do? Why or why not?

2. What do you think about the idea of taking a time out? Is it a good idea to give some space if you are not ready to talk about a specific topic? Do you agree that the person who asks for a time out needs to provide a deadline (i.e., "I'll be ready to talk about it after dinner")? Can you think of a time when the two of you did this? How did it work?

3. If you are both willing, share with the group a topic of conversation that the two of you decided to put on hold (something perhaps that you talked about a million times and still got nowhere). How does it make you feel to do this?

4. Someone said that the best answer to anger is silence. Do you agree? Why or why not? How do you typically respond to anger when it erupts in others (including your partner)?

5. What's your advice quotient? In other words, do you tend to give more of it than you should? And how do you like receiving advice from your partner? When are the times you like it and when do you not like it? Be specific.

Talking through Your Workbook Exercises (10 minutes)

Within your small group, take time to complete Exercise 16 in your workbook, which presents you with some scenarios to determine how you would respond if you were in these situations. After you have completed the exercise, gather back together as a group and answer these questions. What did you learn about yourself from it? Do you agree about the best answer for each of them after you completed it? Why or why not?

Talking Together as a Couple

Spend some time this week doing Exercise 17 and begin delving into the issue of advice giving. So where do you tend to fall on the two advice scales in this exercise? Share with each other what you discovered about yourself. How did you rate each other and what did you learn about each other's advice quotient? Would you be willing to share this with the group next time and explain why you answered the way you did?

Session Six

THE MOST IMPORTANT CONVERSATION YOU'LL EVER HAVE

(Based on chapter 14 in Love Talk*)*

Just for Fun (5 minutes)

If the two of you could strap on jet-propulsion packs that could travel up to 300 miles in a day, how would you use them? You've got twenty-four hours. Where would you go and what would you do with your space-age travel ability?

Video Notes (10–15 minutes)

Talking about Talking (30 minutes)

1. What do you think about the idea that the most important conversation you have each and every day is the conversation you have with yourself? Do you agree or not and why?

2. Imagine the far-fetched notion of being able to electronically tabulate everything you say on a given day about yourself and about your partner and categorize it as either positive or negative. Would you take advantage of this technology if it were actually available? Why or why not?

3. What are some of the most common tapes you play in your head? Can you identify one negative self-statement you tend to repeat and one positive self-statement you also rely on? If you are willing, please share them with the group?

4. Do you agree that self-talk is often believed even if it is irrational? Why or why not? Does one's leaning toward being influenced by facts versus feelings impact this? If so, how does this relate to you specifically?

5. Self-talk is often learned. What are some examples of the tapes (positive or negative) that were implanted in you from the home you grew up in? In what specific ways do they still impact you today?

6. Awareness is curative. Once you become aware of your self-talk, you can do something about it. So what can you do, specifically, now that you are more aware of what you are saying to yourself about you and about your partner? How can you improve your respect levels and influence your "governing relationship message"?

Talking through Your Workbook Exercises (10 minutes)

Within your small group, take time to complete Exercise 18 in your workbook, which will help you tune into your self-talk. What did you learn from your score on this exercise? Knowing that the results are generalizations, what can you gain, in specific terms, about your own tendencies into your self-talk?

Exercise 20 helps you talk from your strengths. This may be one of the most important exercises you have done in this series. Review your Strengths Chart and share with the group a couple of the items you identified as your partner's top mental, social, physical, or spiritual strengths. No need to list them all here. Just select a couple and tell the group why you chose them.

Talking Together as a Couple

Spend some time this week as a couple completing Exercise 19 in this workbook. This exercise will help reveal your respect levels as a couple. Again, talk to the group about what you learned about you and your relationship after completing this self-test. What did you learn from your Partner-Respect Score and your Self-Respect Score?

Love Talk ZondervanGroupware™ Small Group Edition

A Six-Session Guide to Speaking Each Other's Language

Drs. Les and Leslie Parrott

In this six-session Zondervan*Groupware*™ video curriculum, acclaimed relationship experts and real-life couple Les and Leslie Parrott are back with a wonderfully insightful guide for improving the single most important factor in any marriage or love relationship-communication! In *Love Talk*, the Parrotts help participants discover their communication style, their partner's, and how the two can best interact. In this no-nonsense curriculum, "psychobabble" is translated into easy-to-understand language that clearly teaches partners what they need to do-and not do-for healthy communication. Learn how to take your conversations to a deeper level and engage in the most important conversation you and your partner will ever have. Follow the deep and simple plan prescribed in *Love Talk* and begin communicating your way into a happier, healthier, and stronger relationship.

The six sessions include:

1. Communication 101
2. The Foundation of Every Great Conversation
3. Your Personal Talk Style
4. The Secret to Emotional Connection
5. When Not to Talk
6. The Most Important Conversation You'll Ever Have

Designed to be used in conjunction with the Small Group Discussion Guide in the *Love Talk Workbook for Men* and the *Love Talk Workbook for Women*, the DVD package also includes a thirty-two-page leader's guide.

Kit: 0-310-26466-9
DVD: 0-310-26467-7
Booklet: 0-310-26468-5

Love Talk Starters

275 Questions to Get Your Conversations Going

Drs. Les and Leslie Parrott

Acclaimed relationship experts Les and Leslie Parrott are back with a wonderful and insightful guide for improving the single most important factor in any marriage or love relationship—communication. In their book *Love Talk*, the Parrotts help you discover you and your partner's communication style and learn the best ways for your styles to interact. In this companion book, *Love Talk Starters*, you will find engaging, intriguing, and revealing conversation starters. Some questions are just for fun, some will educate you about your spouse's life, and still others will drill down on some more serious topics. Use these simple conversation starters and begin communicating your way into a happier, healthier, and stronger relationship today.

Softcover: 0-310-81047-7

Just the Two of Us
Love Talk Meditations for Couples

Drs. Les and Leslie Parrott

Les and Leslie Parrott share communication insights and wisdom for couples that are newly married or have been married for forty years. The Parrotts write in a very compelling and transparent way using their personal experiences with communication challenges in their own marriage. A wonderful companion to *Love Talk*. Some of the titles of the meditations include: "What Were You Thinking?" "You're Reading My Mind," and "The Talks That Tie Us Together."

Gift book: 0-310-80381-0

Pick up a copy today at your favorite bookstore!

The Love List

Eight Little Things That Make a Big Difference in Your Marriage

Drs. Les and Leslie Parrott

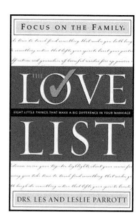

This little book will make a big impact on your marriage. Start right away applying its hands-on concepts. You'll immediately increase intimacy, gain new direction, enjoy more laughter, and much more.

You'll love how the *Love List* unites purposefulness and spontaneity. "A few small actions—practiced on a daily, weekly, monthly, and yearly basis—can change everything for a couple," say relationship experts Les and Leslie Parrott. "Little, deliberate behaviors quietly lavish love on a marriage."

Drawing on their professional insights into successful couples and sharing candidly from their own marriage, the Parrotts give you eight simple-but-powerful, instantly usable principles that will lift your marriage out of the doldrums into everything you've wanted it to be. Plus, it's also fun! Especially when you start seeing noticeable results right away.

Hardcover: 0-310-24850-7

Pick up a copy today at your favorite bookstore!

ZONDERVAN®
.com

Saving Your Marriage Before It Starts

Seven Questions to Ask Before—and After—You Marry

Drs. Les and Leslie Parrott

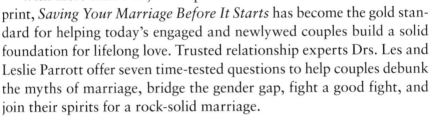

A trusted marriage resource for engaged and newlywed couples is now expanded and updated.

With more than 500,000 copies in print, *Saving Your Marriage Before It Starts* has become the gold standard for helping today's engaged and newlywed couples build a solid foundation for lifelong love. Trusted relationship experts Drs. Les and Leslie Parrott offer seven time-tested questions to help couples debunk the myths of marriage, bridge the gender gap, fight a good fight, and join their spirits for a rock-solid marriage.

This expanded and updated edition of *Saving Your Marriage Before It Starts* has been honed by ten years of feedback, professional experience, research, and insight, making this tried-and-true resource better than ever. Specifically designed to meet the needs of today's couples, this book equips readers for a lifelong marriage before it even starts.

The men's and women's workbooks include self-tests and exercises sure to bring about personal insight and help you apply what you learn. The seven-session DVD features the Parrotts' lively presentation as well as real-life couples, making this a tool you can use "right out of the box." Two additional sessions for second marriages are also included. The unabridged audio CD is read by the authors.

The Curriculum Kit includes DVD with Leader's Guide, hardcover book, workbooks for men and women, and *Saving Your Second Marriage Before It Starts* workbooks for men and women. All components, except for DVD, are also sold separately.

Curriculum Kit   0-310-27180-0

Also Available:

0-310-26210-0	Saving Your Marriage Before It Starts	Audio CD, Unabridged
0-310-26565-7	Saving Your Marriage Before It Starts Workbook for Men	Softcover
0-310-26564-9	Saving Your Marriage Before It Starts Workbook for Women	Softcover
0-310-27585-7	Saving Your Second Marriage Before It Starts Workbook for Women	Softcover
0-310-27584-9	Saving Your Second Marriage Before It Starts Workbook for Men	Softcover

Saving Your Second Marriage Before It Starts

Nine Questions to Ask Before (and After) You Remarry

Drs. Les and Leslie Parrott

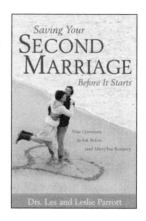

Sixty percent of second marriages fail. Yours can be among the ones that succeed. Relationship experts Les and Leslie Parrott show how you can beat the odds with flying colors and make remarriage the best thing that's ever happened to you. Do you have the skills you need? Now is the time to acquire them—and build a future together that is everything marriage can and ought to be.

Also available: men's workbook, women's workbook, and abridged audio cassette version

Hardcover, Jacketed   0-310-20748-7

Also Available:

0-310-24054-9	Saving Your Second Marriage Before It Starts Workbook for Men	Softcover
0-310-24055-7	Saving Your Second Marriage Before It Starts Workbook for Women	Softcover

Pick up a copy today at your favorite bookstore!

Becoming Soul Mates

Les and Leslie Parrott

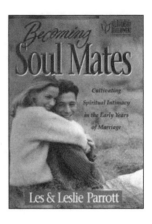

Every couple has a restless aching, not just to know God individually but to experience God together. But how? How do you really allow God to fill the soul of your marriage?

Becoming Soul Mates gives you a road map for cultivating rich spiritual intimacy in your relationship. Written by the creators of the dynamic *Saving Your Marriage Before It Starts* book and program, *Becoming Soul Mates* is a unique and insightful devotional that helps you dig deep for a strong spiritual foundation in your marriage. Fifty-two practical weekly devotions help you and your partner cross the hurdles of marriage to grow closer than you've ever imagined.

In each session you'll find:

- An insightful devotion that focuses on marriage-related topics
- A key passage of Scripture
- Questions that will spark discussions on crucial issues
- Insights from real-life soul mates
- A brief prayer that will help you both draw closer together and close to God

Becoming Soul Mates is a valuable resource for mining the rich potential of your relationship. Its principles, proven in the Parrotts' own relationship, will help you make your journey as a couple all God intends it to be. With the strength that comes from a deeply shared spiritual intimacy, your marriage can flourish in the midst of life's challenges. Start building on the closeness you've got today—and reap the rewards of a deeper, more satisfying relationship in the years ahead.

Also Available
0-310-21926-4   Becoming Soul Mates   Softcover

Pick up a copy today at your favorite bookstore!

The Complete Guide to Marriage Mentoring

Connecting Couples to Build Better Marriages

Drs. Les and Leslie Parrott

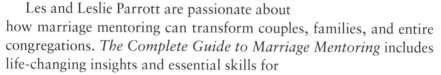

A comprehensive resource to help churches build a thriving marriage mentoring program.

Les and Leslie Parrott are passionate about how marriage mentoring can transform couples, families, and entire congregations. *The Complete Guide to Marriage Mentoring* includes life-changing insights and essential skills for

- Preparing engaged and newlywed couples
- Maximizing marriages from good to great
- Repairing marriages in distress

Practical guidelines help mentors and couples work together as a team, agree on outcomes, and develop skills for the marriage mentoring process. Appendixes offer a wealth of additional resources and tools. An exhaustive resource for marriage mentorship in any church setting, this guide also includes insights from interviews with church leaders and marriage mentors from around the country.

> "The time is ripe for marriage mentoring, and this book is exactly what we need."
> **— GARY SMALLEY, AUTHOR OF *THE DNA OF RELATIONSHIPS***

Hardcover, Printed   0-310-27046-4

Also Available:

0-310-27047-2	51 Creative Ideas for Marriage Mentors	Softcover
0-310-27110-X	Complete Resource Kit for Marriage Mentoring, The	Curriculum Kit
0-310-27165-7	Marriage Mentor Training Manual for Husbands	Softcover
0-310-27125-8	Marriage Mentor Training Manual for Wives	Softcover

Pick up a copy today at your favorite bookstore!

We want to hear from you. Please send your comments about this book to us in care of zreview@zondervan.com. Thank you.

ZONDERVAN.com/
AUTHORTRACKER
follow your favorite authors